KADARAM KONDAN

THE UNTOLD STORY OF RAJENDRA CHOLA

KAVEEN

Contents

Contents

CHAPTER ONE

INTRODUCTION

The region of Tamil Nadu or Tamilakam, in the southeast of modern India, shows evidence of having had continuous human habitation from 15,000 BCE to 10,000 BCE. Throughout its history, spanning the early Upper Paleolithic age to modern times, this region has coexisted with various external cultures. The three ancient Tamil dynasties namely Chera, Chola, and Pandya were of ancient origins. Together they ruled over this land with a unique culture and language, contributing to the growth of some of the oldest extant literature in the world. These three dynasties were in constant struggle with each other vying for hegemony over the land. Invasion by the Kalabhras during the 3rd century disturbed the traditional order of the land, displacing the three ruling kingdoms. These occupiers were overthrown by the resurgence of the Pandyas and the Pallavas, who restored the traditional kingdoms. The Cholas who re-emerged from obscurity in the 9th century by defeating the Pallavas and the Pandyas rose to become a great power and extended their empire over the entire southern peninsula.] At its height the Chola empire spanned almost 3,600,000 km² (1,389,968 sq mi) straddling the Bay of Bengal.The Chola navy held sway over the Sri Vijaya kingdom in Southeast Asia. Rapid changes in the political situation of the rest of India occurred due to incursions of Muslim armies from the northwest and the decline of the three ancient dynasties during the 14th century, the Tamil country became part of the Vijayanagara Empire. Under this empire, the Telugu speaking Nayak governors ruled before the European trading companies appeared during the 17th century eventually assuming greater sway over the indigenous rulers of the land. The Madras Presidency, comprising most of southern India, was created in the 18th century and was ruled directly by the British. After the independence of India, after the Telugu and Malayalam parts of Madras state were separated from Tamilakam state in 1956, it was renamed as Tamil Nadu in 1969 by the state government. Ancient Tamil Nadu contained three monarchical states, headed by kings called Vendhar and several tribal chieftaincies, headed by the chiefs called by the general denomination Vel or Velir. Still lower at the local level there were clan chiefs called kizhar or mannar. During the 3rd century BCE, the Deccan was part of the Maurya Empire, and from the middle of the 1st century BCE to 2nd century CE the same area was ruled by the Satavahana dynasty. The Tamil area had an independent existence outside the control of these northern empires. The Tamil kings and chiefs were always in conflict with each other mostly over the property. The royal courts were mostly places of social gathering rather than places of dispensation of authority; they were centres for distribution of resources. Tamil literature Tolkappiyam sheds some light on early religion. Gradually the rulers came under the influence of Vedic beliefs, which encouraged performance of sacrifices to enhance the status of the ruler. Buddhism, Jainism and Ajivika coexisted with early Shaivite, Vaishnavism and Shaktism during the first five centuries. The names of the three dynasties, Cholas, Pandyas, and Cheras, are mentioned in the Pillars of Ashoka (inscribed 273–232 BCE) inscriptions, among the kingdoms, which though not subject to Ashoka, were on friendly terms with him. The king of Kalinga, Kharavela, who ruled around 150 BCE, mentioned in the famous Hathigumpha inscription of the confederacy of the Tamil kingdoms that had existed for over 100 years. Karikala Chola was the most famous early Chola. He is mentioned in a number of poems in the Sangam poetry.[27] In later times Karikala was the subject of many legends found in the Cilappatikaram and in inscriptions and literary works of the 11th and 12th centuries. They attribute to him the conquest of the whole of India up to the Himalayas and the construction of the flood banks of the river Kaveri with the aid of his feudatories. These legends, however, are conspicuous by their absence in the Sangam poetry. Kocengannan was another famous early Chola king who has been extolled in a number of poems of the Sangam period. He was even made a Saiva saint during the medieval period. Pandyas ruled initially from Korkai, a seaport on the southernmost tip of the Indian peninsula, and in later times moved to Madurai. Pandyas are also mentioned in Sangam Literature, as well as by Greek and Roman sources during this period. Megasthenes in his Indika mentions the Pandyan kingdom. The Pandyas controlled the present districts of Madurai, Tirunelveli, and parts of south Kerala. They had trading contacts with Greece and Rome. With the other kingdoms of Tamilakam, they maintained trading contacts and marital relationships with Tamil merchants from Eelam. Various Pandya kings find mention in a number of poems in the Sangam literature. Among them, Nedunjeliyan, 'the victor of Talaiyalanganam' deserves a special mention. Besides several short poems found in the Akananuru and the Purananuru collections, there are two major works—Mathuraikkanci and the Netunalvatai (in the collection of Pattupattu) that give a glimpse into the society and commercial activities in the Pandyan kingdom during the Sangam age. The early Pandyas went into obscurity at the end of the 3rd century CE during the incursion of the Kalabhras. The kingdom of the Cheras comprised the modern Western Tamil Nadu and Kerala, along the western or Malabar Coast of southern India. Their proximity to the sea favoured trade with Africa. Chera rulers dated to the first few centuries AD. It records the names of the kings, the princes, and the court poets who extolled them. The internal chronology of this literature is still far from settled, and at present, a connected account of the history of the period cannot be derived. Uthiyan Cheralathan, Nedum Cheralathan and Senguttuvan Chera are some of the rulers referred to in the Sangam poems. Senguttuvan Chera, the most celebrated Chera king, is famous for the legends surrounding Kannagi, the heroine of the Tamil epic Silapathikaram. These early kingdoms sponsored the growth of some of the oldest extant literature in Tamil. The classical Tamil literature, referred to as Sangam literature is attributed to the period between 500 BCE and 300 CE. The poems of Sangam literature, which deal with emotional and material topics, were categorised and collected into various anthologies during the medieval period. These Sangam poems paint the picture of a fertile land and of a people who were organised into various occupational groups. The governance of the land was through hereditary monarchies, although the sphere of the state's activities and the extent of the ruler's powers were limited through the adherence to the established order (dharma). The people were loyal to their kings and roving bards and musicians and danseuse gathered at the royal courts of the generous kings. The arts of music and dancing were highly developed and popular. Musical instruments of various types find mention in the Sangam poems. The amalgamation of the southern and the northern styles of dancing started during this period and is reflected fully in the epic Cilappatikaram. Internal and external trade was well organised and active. Evidence from both archaeology and literature speaks of a flourishing foreign trade with the Yavanas (Greeks). The port city of Puhar on the east coast and Muziris on the west coast of south India were emporia of foreign trade, where huge ships moored, offloading precious merchandise. [39] This trade started to decline after the 2nd century CE and the direct contact between the Roman empire and the ancient Tamil country was replaced by trade with the Arabs and the Auxumites of East Africa. Internal trade was also brisk and goods were sold and bartered. Agriculture was the main profession of a vast majority of the populace.

DARK AGE

After the close of the Sangam era, from about 300 to about 600 CE, there is an almost total lack of information regarding occurrences in the Tamil land. Some time about 300 CE, the whole region was upset by the appearance of the Kalabhras. These people are described in later literature as 'evil rulers' who overthrew the established Tamil kings and got a stranglehold of the country. information about their origin and details about their reign is scarce. They did not leave many artifacts or monuments. The only source of information on them is the scattered mentions in Buddhist and Jain literature. Historians speculate that these people followed Buddhist or Jain faiths and were antagonistic towards the Hindu religions (viz. the Astika schools) adhered by the majority of inhabitants of the Tamil region during the early centuries CE . As a result, Hindu scholars and authors who followed their decline in the 7th and 8th century may have expunged any mention of them in their texts and generally tended to paint their rule in a negative light. It is perhaps due to this reason, the period of their rule is known as a 'Dark Age'—an interregnum. Some of the ruling families migrated northwards and found enclaves for themselves away from the Kalabhras. Jainism and Buddhism took deep roots in the society, giving birth to a large body of ethical poetry. Writing became very widespread and vatteluttu evolved from the Tamil-Brahmi became a mature script for writing Tamil. While several anthologies were compiled by collecting bardic poems of earlier centuries, some of the epic poems such as the Cilappatikaram and didactic works such as the Tirukkural were also written during this period.[46] The patronage of the Jain and Buddhist scholars by the Kalabhra kings influenced the nature of the literature of the period, and most of the works that can be attributed to this period were written by the Jain and Buddhist authors. In the field of dance and music, the elite started patronising new polished styles, partly influenced by northern ideas, in the place of the folk styles. A few of the earliest rock-cut temples belong to this period. Brick temples (known as kottam, devakulam, and palli) dedicated to various deities are referred to in literary works. Kalabhras were displaced around the 7th century by the revival of Pallava and Pandya power. Even with the exit of the Kalabhras, the Jain and Buddhist influence still remained in Tamil Nadu. The early Pandya and the Pallava kings were followers of these faiths. The Hindu reaction to this apparent decline of their religion was growing and reached its peak during the later part of the 7th century. There was a widespread Hindu revival during which a huge body of Saiva and Vaishnava literature was created. Many Saiva Nayanmars and Vaishnava Alvars provided a great stimulus to the growth of popular devotional literature. Karaikkal Ammaiyar who lived in the 6th century CE was the earliest of these Nayanmars. The celebrated Saiva hymnists Sundaramurthi, Thirugnana Sambanthar and Thirunavukkarasar were of this period. Vaishnava Alvars such as Poigai Alvar, Bhoothathalvar and Peyalvar produced devotional hymns for their faith and their songs were collected later into the four thousand poems of Naalayira Divyap Prabhandham.

• 8 •

CHAPTER THREE

AGE OF EMPIRES
600-1300 BC

The medieval period of the history of the Tamil country saw the rise and fall of many kingdoms, some of whom went on to the extent of empires, exerting influences both in India and overseas. The Cholas who were very active during the Sangam age were entirely absent during the first few centuries. The period started with the rivalry between the Pandyas and the Pallavas, which in turn caused the revival of the Cholas. The Cholas went on to becoming a great power. Their decline saw the brief resurgence of the Pandyas. This period was also that of the re-invigorated Hinduism during which temple building and religious literature were at their best. The Hindu sects Saivism and Vaishnavism became dominant, replacing the prevalence of Jainism and Buddhism of the previous era. Saivism was patronised more by the Chola kings and became more or less a state religion. Some of the earliest temples that are still standing were built during this period by the Pallavas. The rock-cut temples in Mamallapuram and the majestic Kailasanatha and Vaikuntaperumal temples of Kanchipuram stand testament to the Pallava art. The Cholas, utilising their prodigious wealth earned through their extensive conquests, built long-lasting stone temples including the great Brihadisvara temple of Thanjavur and exquisite bronze sculptures. Temples dedicated to Siva and Vishnu received liberal donations of money, jewels, animals, and land, and thereby became powerful economic institutions. Tamil script replaced the vatteluttu script throughout Tamil Nadu for writing Tamil. Religious literature flourished during the period. The Tamil epic, Kamban's Ramavatharam, was written in the 13th century. A contemporary of Kamban was the famous poet Auvaiyar who found great happiness in writing for young children. The secular literature was mostly court poetry devoted to the eulogy of the rulers. The religious poems of the previous period and the classical literature of the Sangam period were collected and systematised into several anthologies. Sanskrit was patronised by the priestly groups for religious rituals and other ceremonial purposes. Nambi Andar Nambi, who was a contemporary of Rajaraja Chola I, collected and arranged the books on Saivism into eleven books called Tirumurais. The hagiology of Saivism was standardised in Periyapuranam by Sekkilar, who lived during the reign of Kulothunga Chola II (1133–1150 CE). Jayamkondar's Kalingattupparani, a semi-historical account on the two invasions of Kalinga by Kulothunga Chola I was an early example of a biographical work.

CHAPTER FOUR

CHOLAS

Around 850, out of obscurity rose Vijayalaya, made use of an opportunity arising out of a conflict between Pandyas and Pallavas, captured Thanjavur from Mutharaiyar dynasty and eventually established the imperial line of the medieval Cholas. Vijayalaya revived the Chola dynasty and his son Aditya I helped establish their independence. He invaded Pallava kingdom in 903 and killed the Pallava king Aparajita in battle, ending the Pallava reign. The Chola kingdom under Parantaka I expanded to cover the entire Pandya country. However, towards the end of his reign, he suffered several reverses by the Rashtrakutas who had extended their territories well into the Chola kingdom. The Cholas went into a temporary decline during the next few years due to weak kings, palace intrigues and succession disputes. Despite a number of attempts, the Pandya country could not be completely subdued and the Rashtrakutas were still a powerful enemy in the north. However, the Chola revival began with the accession of Rajaraja Chola I in 985. Cholas rose as a notable military, economic and cultural power in Asia under Rajaraja and his son Rajendra Chola I. The Chola territories stretched from the islands of Maldives in the south to as far north as the banks of the river Ganges in Bengal. Rajaraja Chola conquered peninsular South India, annexed parts of Sri Lanka and occupied the islands of Maldives. Rajendra Chola extended the Chola conquests to the Malayan archipelago by defeating the Srivijaya kingdom.[65] He defeated Mahipala, the king of Bihar and Bengal, and to commemorate his victory he built a new capital called Gangaikonda Cholapuram (the town of Cholas who conquered the Ganges). At its peak, the Chola Empire extended from the island of Sri Lanka in the south to the Godavari basin in the north. The kingdoms along the east coast of India up to the river Ganges acknowledged Chola suzerainty. Chola navies invaded and conquered Srivijaya in the Malayan archipelago. Chola armies exacted tribute from Thailand and the Khmer kingdom of Cambodia. During the reign of Rajaraja and Rajendra, the administration of the Chola empire matured considerably. The empire was divided into a number of self-governing local government units, and the officials were selected through a system of popular elections. Throughout this period, the Cholas were constantly troubled by the ever-resilient Sinhalas trying to overthrow the Chola occupation of Lanka, Pandya princes trying to win independence for their traditional territories, and by the growing ambitions of the Chalukyas in the western Deccan. The history of this period was one of constant warfare between the Cholas and of these antagonists. A balance of power existed between the Chalukyas and the Cholas and there was a tacit acceptance of the Tungabhadra river as the boundary between the two empires. However, the bone of contention between these two powers was the growing Chola influence in the Vengi kingdom. The Cholas and Chalukyas fought many battles and both kingdoms were exhausted by the endless battles and a stalemate existed. Marital and political alliances between the Eastern Chalukya kings based around Vengi located on the south banks of the river Godavari began during the reign of Rajaraja following his invasion of Vengi. Virarajendra Chola's son Athirajendra Chola was assassinated in a civil disturbance in 1070 and Kulothunga Chola I ascended the Chola throne starting the Chalukya Chola dynasty. Kulothunga was a son of the Vengi king Rajaraja Narendra. The Chalukya Chola dynasty saw very capable rulers in Kulothunga Chola I and Vikrama Chola, however, the eventual decline of the Chola power practically started during this period. The Cholas lost control of the island of Lanka and were driven out by the revival of Sinhala power. Around 1118 they also lost the control of Vengi to Western Chalukya king Vikramaditya VI and Gangavadi (southern Mysore districts) to the growing power of Hoysala Vishnuvardhana, a Chalukya feudatory. In the Pandya territories, the lack of a controlling central administration caused a number of claimants to the Pandya throne to cause a civil war in which the Sinhalas and the Cholas were involved by proxy. During the last century of the Chola existence, a permanent Hoysala army was stationed in Kanchipuram to protect them from the growing influence of the Pandyas. Rajendra Chola III was the last Chola king. The Kadava chieftain Kopperunchinga I even captured Rajendra and held him prisoner. At the close of Rajendra's reign (1279), the Pandyan empire was at the height of prosperity and had completely absorbed the Chola kingdom. The Cholas also found a place in the very famous novel by Kalki title Ponniyin Selvan which portrays the whole Chola history with Rajaraja Cholan (Ponniyin Selvan, Arul Mozhi Varman, Vallavarayan Vanthiyaththevan, Karikalar, Nandhini, Kundhavi) as the characters of the novel. The

Chola dynasty was a Tamil dynasty of southern India, one of the longest-ruling dynasties in the world's history. The earliest datable references to the Chola are in inscriptions from the 3rd century BCE left by Ashoka, of the Maurya Empire (Ashoka Major Rock Edict No.13). As one of the Three Crowned Kings of Tamilakam, along with the Chera and Pandya, the dynasty continued to govern over varying territory until the 13th century CE. Despite these ancient origins, the period when it is appropriate to speak of a "Chola Empire" only begins with the medieval Cholas in the mid-9th century CE.

- *Vijayalaya 848–891*
- *Aditya I-891–907*
- *Parantaka I-907–950*
- *Gandaraditya-950–957*
- *Arinjaya-956–957*
- *Sundara (Parantaka II)-957–970*
- *Aditya II-(co-regent)*
- *Uttama-970–985*
- *Rajaraja I-985–1014*
- *Rajendra I-1012–1044*
- *Rajadhiraja-1044–1054*
- *Rajendra II-1054–1063*
- *Virarajendra-1063–1070*
- *Athirajendra-1070–1070*
- **<u>Later Cholas</u>**
- *Kulothunga I1070–1120*
- *Vikrama 1118–1135*
- *Kulothunga II 1133–1150*
- *Rajaraja II 1146–1173*
- *Rajadhiraja II 1166–1178*
- *Kulothunga III 1178–1218*

- *Rajaraja III 1216–1256*
- *III Rajendra 1246–1279*

CHAPTER FIVE

THE CHOLA EMPIRE

The genealogy of the Chola empire as found in the Tamil literature and in the many inscriptions left by the later Chola kings contains a number of kings recorded for whom there is no verifiable historic evidence. There are as many versions of this lineage as there are sources for them. The main source is the Sangam literature – particularly, religious literature such as Periapuranam, semi-biographical poems of the later Chola period such as the temple and cave inscription and left by medieval Cholas.

Irrespective of the source, no list of the kings has a high level of historic fact and, while they generally are similar to each other, no two lists are exactly the same. Modern historians[who?] consider these lists not as historically reliable sources but as comprehensive conglomerations of various Hindu deities and Puranic characters attributed to local chieftains and invented ancestry of dynasty attempting to re-establish their legitimacy and supremacy in a land they were trying to conquer.

CHAPTER SIX

THE PREHISTORICAL CHOLAS

A number of typical hero and demi-gods found their place in the ancestry claimed by the later Cholas in the long typical genealogies incorporated into the copper-plate charters and stone inscription of the tenth and eleventh centuries. The earliest version of this is found in the kilbil Plates which gives fifteen names before Chola including the genuinely historical ones of Karikala, Perunarkilli and Kocengannan. The Thiruvalangadu Plate swells this list to forty-four, and the Kanya Plate runs up to fifty-two. The Cholas were looked upon as descended from the sun. These myths speak of a Chola king, supposed contemporary of the sage Agastya, whose devotion brought the river Kavery into existence. There is also the story of the king Manu Needhi Cholan who sentenced his son to death for having accidentally killed a calf. He was called thus because he followed the rules of Manu; his real name is not mentioned and is thought to be Ellalan according to Maha vamsam who was also attributed with a similar story. King Shivi who rescued a dove from a hunter by giving his own flesh to the hungry and poor hunter was also part of the early Chola legends. King Shivi was also called Sembiyan, a popular title assumed by a number of Chola kings.

CHOLAS OF SANGAM PERIOD

The early Chola kings of the Sangam period and the life of people contributed much to the cultural wealth of the Tamil country. The Sangam literature is full of legends about the mythical Chola kings.

CHAPTER EIGHT

GENEALOGY OF CHOLA INSCRIPTIONS

The genealogy of the Chola family conveyed by the Thiruvalangadu copperplate grant consists of names that corroborate the historic authenticity of legends.The heartland of the Cholas was the fertile valley of the Kaveri River, but they ruled a significantly larger area at the height of their power from the later half of the 9th century till the beginning of the 13th century. The whole country south of the Tungabhadra was united and held as one state for a period of three centuries and more between 907 and 1215 AD. Under Rajaraja Chola I and his successors Rajendra Chola I, Rajadhiraja Chola, Virarajendra Chola, and Kulothunga Chola I, the dynasty became a military, economic and cultural power in South Asia and South-East Asia. The power of the new empire was proclaimed to the eastern world by the expedition to the Ganges which Rajendra Chola I undertook and by naval raids on cities of the city-state of Srivijaya, as well as by the repeated embassies to China.he Chola fleet represented the zenith of ancient Indian sea power. During the period 1010–1153, the Chola territories stretched from the islands of the Maldives in the south to as far north as the banks of the

Godavari River in Andhra Pradesh. Rajaraja Chola conquered peninsular South India, annexed parts of which is now Sri Lanka and occupied the islands of the Maldives. Rajendra Chola sent a victorious expedition to North India that touched the river Ganges and defeated the Pala ruler of Pataliputra, Mahipala. He also successfully invaded cities of Srivijaya of Malaysia and Indonesia. The Chola dynasty went into decline at the beginning of the 13th century with the rise of the Pandyan dynasty, which ultimately caused their downfall. The Cholas left a lasting legacy. Their patronage of Tamil literature and their zeal in the building of temples has resulted in some great works of Tamil literature and architecture. The Chola kings were avid builders and envisioned the temples in their kingdoms not only as places of worship but also as centres of economic activity. They pioneered a centralised form of government and established a disciplined bureaucracy. The Chola school of art spread to Southeast Asia and influenced the architecture and art of Southeast Asia.

CHAPTER NINE

ORGINS

The Cholas are also known as the Choda. The antiquity of the name is evident from the mentions in ancient Tamil literature and in inscriptions. During the past 150 years, historians have gleaned significant knowledge on the subject from a variety of sources such as ancient Tamil Sangam literature, oral traditions, religious texts, temple and copperplate inscriptions. The main source for the available information of the early Cholas is the early Tamil literature of the Sangam Period. Mentions in the early Sangam literature (c. 150 CE) indicate that the earliest kings of the dynasty antedated 100 CE. There are also brief notices on the Chola country and its towns, ports and commerce furnished by the Periplus of the Erythraean Sea (Periplus Maris Erythraei), and in the slightly later work of the geographer Ptolemy. Mahavamsa, a Buddhist text written down during the 5th century CE, recounts a number of conflicts between the inhabitants of Ceylon and Cholas in the 1st century BCE. Cholas are mentioned in the Pillars of Ashoka (inscribed 273 BCE–232 BCE) inscriptions, where they are mentioned among the kingdoms which, though not subject to Ashoka, were on friendly terms with him. A commonly held view is that Chola is, like Chera and Pandya, the name of the ruling family or clan of immemorial antiquity. The annotator Parimelazhagar said: "The charity of people with ancient lineage (such as the Cholas, the Pandyas and the Cheras) are forever generous in spite of their reduced means". The imperial Cholas described themselves as Koliyar-ko, meaning king of Koliyar in Tamil. Gandaraditya Chola, considered the author of some of the hymns of the Tirumurai, calls himself as "Ko-cholan valan kaveri naadan Koliyar-ko kandan", that is, "Gandan, the King Cholan, the lord of the fertile kaveri country and the lord of Koliyar". Vikrama Chola, the son of Kulothunga Chola and a later Chola king, is described as Koliyar kula Pati or "head of the family of Cholas" in one of his Tamil inscriptions in Kolar district in Karnataka. The koliyar were one of the artisan communities during the period of the Cholas. Some historians like Vijaya Ramasamy, consider the koliyar to be weavers.

CHAPTER TEN

THE HISTORY OF CHOLA FALLS INTO 4 PERIODS

The Early Cholas of the Sangam literature, the interregnum between the fall of the Sangam Cholas and the rise of the Imperial medieval Around the 7th century, a Chola kingdom flourished in present-day Andhra Pradesh. These Telugu Cholas traced their descent to the early Sangam Cholas. However, it is not known if they had any relation to the early Cholas. It is possible that a branch of the Tamil Cholas migrated north during the time of the Pallavas to establish a kingdom of their own, away from the dominating influences of the Pandyas and Pallavas. The Chinese pilgrim Xuanzang, who spent several months in Kanchipuram during 639–640 writes about the "kingdom of Culi-ya", in an apparent reference to these Telugu Cholas.

CHAPTER ELEVEN

IMPERIAL CHOLAS

Vijayalaya was the founder of the Imperial Chola dynasty which was the beginning of one of the most splendid empires in Indian history. Vijayalaya, possibly a feudatory of the Pallava dynasty, took an opportunity arising out of a conflict between the Pandya dynasty and Pallava dynasty in c. 850, captured Thanjavur from Muttarayar, and established the imperial line of the medieval Chola Dynasty. Thanjavur became the capital of the Imperial Chola Dynasty.The Chola dynasty was at the peak of its influence and power during the medieval period. Through their leadership and vision, Chola kings expanded their territory and influence. The second Chola King, Aditya I, caused the demise of the Pallava dynasty and defeated the Pandyan dynasty of Madurai in 885, occupied large parts of the Kannada country, and had marital ties with the Western Ganga dynasty. In 925, his son Parantaka I conquered Sri Lanka (known as Ilangai). Parantaka I also defeated the Rashtrakuta dynasty under Krishna II in the battle of Vallala. Rajaraja Chola I and Rajendra Chola I were the greatest rulers of the Chola dynasty, extending it beyond the traditional limits of a Tamil kingdom. At its peak, the Chola Empire stretched from the island of Sri Lanka in the south to the Godavari-Krishna river basin in the north, up to the Konkan coast in Bhatkal, the entire Malabar Coast (the Chea country) in addition to Lakshadweep, and Maldives. Rajaraja Chola I was a ruler with inexhaustible energy, and he applied himself to the task of governance with the same zeal that he had shown in waging wars. He integrated his empire into a tight administrative grid under royal control, and at the same time strengthened local self-government. Therefore, he conducted a land survey in 1000 CE to effectively marshall the resources of his empire.

Rajendra Chola I conquered Odisha and his armies continued to march further north and defeated the forces of the Pala Dynasty of Bengal and reached the Ganges river in north India. Rajendra Chola I built a new capital called Gangaikonda Cholapuram to celebrate his victories in northern India. Rajendra Chola I successfully invaded the Srivijaya kingdom in Southeast Asia which led to the decline of the empire there. This expedition had such a great impression to the Malay people of the medieval period that his name was mentioned in the corrupted form as Raja Chulan in the medieval Malay chronicle Sejarah Melayu. He also completed the conquest of the island of Sri Lanka and took the Sinhala king Mahinda V as a prisoner, in addition to his conquests of Rattapadi (territories of the Rashtrakutas, Chalukya country, Talakkad, and Kolar, where the Kolaramma temple still has his portrait statue) in Kannada country. Rajendra's territories included the area falling on the Ganges-Hooghly-Damodar basin, as well as Sri Lanka and Maldives. The kingdoms along the east coast of India up to the river Ganges acknowledged Chola suzerainty.T hree diplomatic missions were sent to China in 1016, 1033, and 1077.

CHAPTER TWELVE

OVERSEAS CONQUESTS

During the reign of Rajaraja Chola I and his successors Rajendra Chola I, Virarajendra Chola and Kulothunga Chola I the Chola armies invaded Sri Lanka, the Maldives and parts of Southeast Asia like Malaysia, Indonesia and Southern Thailand of the Srivijaya Empire in the 11th century. Rajaraja Chola I launched several naval campaigns that resulted in the capture of Sri Lanka, Maldives and the Malabar Coast. In 1025, Rajendra Chola launched naval raids on ports of Srivijaya and against the Burmese kingdom of Pegu. A Chola inscription states that he captured or plundered 14 places, which have been identified with Palembang, Tambralinga and Kedah among others.

CHAPTER THIRTEEN

TAMBRALINGA [OR] KADARAM IN TAMIL

According to the inscription no.24 found at Hua-wieng temple in Chaiya near to Nakhon Si Thammarat, the ruler of Tambralinga named Chandrabhanu Sridhamaraja was the king of Patama vamsa (lotus dynasty. He began to reign in 1230, he had the Phrae Boromadhatu (chedi in Nakhon Si Thammaraj, from Sanskrit dhatu - element, component, or relic + garbha - storehouse or repository) reparation and celebration in the same year. Chandrabhanu Sridhamaraja brought Tambralinga reached the pinnacle of its power in the mid-thirteenth century. From the Sri Lankan and Tamil materials, this Chandrabhanu was a Savakan king from Tambralinga who had invaded Sri Lanka in 1247. His navy launched an assault on the southern part of the island but was defeated by the Sri Lankan king. However Chandrabhanu was able to establish an independent regime in the north of the island over the Jaffna kingdom, but in 1258 he was attacked and subjugated by the south Indian Emperor Jatavarman Sundara Pandyan. He was compelled to pay a tribute to the Pandyan Dynasty of precious jewels and elephants. In 1262 Chandrabhanu launched another attack on the south of the island, his army strengthened this time by the addition of Tamil and Sinhalese forces, only to be defeated when Pandya sided with the Sri Lankan side; this time Jatarvarman Sundara Pandyan's brother Jatavarman Veera Pandyan intervened and Chandrabhanu himself was killed in the fighting. Chandrabhanu's son Savakanmaindan inherited the throne and submitted to Veera Pandyan's rule, received rewards and retained control over the northern kingdom. His regime too had disappeared following Maravarman Kulasekara Pandyan I's ascension to the Pandyan empire's throne and another invasion of the island by the army of the Pandyan Dynasty in the late 1270s. Maravarman Kulasekara Pandyan I installed his minister in charge of the invasion, Kulasekara Cinkaiariyan, an Aryachakravarti as the new king of Jaffna. In at least two senses, the rapid expansion of Tambralinga is exceptional in the history of Southeast Asia. In the first place, Candrabhanu's invasion of Sri Lanka and occupation of the Jaffna kingdom marks the only time that a Southeast Asian power has launched an overseas military expedition beyond the immediate Southeast Asian region. In the second place, in the historiography of Southeast Asia the southern Thailand has generally played a secondary role to that of places like Java, the Malacca Strait region (Srivijaya in the seventh~eighth century, Melaka in the fifteenth century), Cambodia, Champa, Vietnam, and Burma. Tambralinga's sudden appearance on centre-stage in the thirteenth century was thus highly unusual. By the end of the fourteenth century, Tambralinga had been submerged by the Sumatran Melayu Kingdom which had the backing of Java. Finally, in 1365 Majapahit Kingdom of Java recognized Nakorn Sri Dharmaraja as Dharmanagari written in Nagarakretagama. Despite its rapid rise to prominence in the thirteenth century, that is, by the following century

Danmaling, or Tambralinga, the former member state of Sanfoshih – Javaka, had become a part of Siam.

KEDAH

A second invasion was led by Virarajendra Chola, who conquered Kedah in Malaysia of Srivijaya in the late 11th century. also known by its honorific Darul Aman or "Abode of Peace is a state of Malaysia, located in the northwestern part of Peninsular Malaysia. The state covers a total area of over 9,000 km², and it consists of the mainland and the Langkawi islands. The mainland has a relatively flat terrain, which is used to grow rice, while Langkawi is an archipelago, most of which are uninhabited islands. Kedah was previously known as Kadaram (Tamil: கடாரம்; kadāram) by the ancient and medieval Tamils. To the north, Kedah borders the state of Perlis and shares an international boundary with the Songkhla and Yala provinces of Thailand. It borders the states of Perak to the south and Penang to the southwest. The state's capital is Alor Setar and the royal seat is in Anak Bukit. Other major towns include Sungai Petani, and Kulim on the mainland, and Kuah on Langkawi. Chola invasion ultimately failed to install direct administration over Srivijaya, since the invasion was short and only meant to plunder the wealth of Srivijaya. However, this invasion gravely weakened the Srivijayan hegemony and enabled the formation of regional kingdoms. Although the invasion was not followed by direct Cholan occupation and the region was unchanged geographically, there were huge consequences in trade. Tamil traders encroached on the Srivijayan realm traditionally controlled by Malay traders and the Tamil guilds' influence increased on the Malay Peninsula and north coast of Sumatra.

CHAPTER FIFTEEN

CHOLA INVASION OF SRIVIJAYA

In 1025, Rajendra Chola I or Raja Ranganathan, the Chola king from Tamil Nadu in South India, launched naval raids on the city-state of Srivijaya in maritime Southeast Asia, and conquered Kadaram (modern Kedah) from Srivijaya and occupied it for some time. Rajendra's overseas expedition against Srivijaya was a unique event in India's history and its otherwise peaceful relations with the states of Southeast Asia. Several places in present day Malaysia and Indonesia were invaded by Rajendra Chola I of the Chola dynasty. The Chola invasion furthered the expansion of Tamil merchant associations such as the Manigramam, Ayyavole and Ainnurruvar into Southeast Asia. (See Chapetr ... on Tamil M erchants of Ancient India) The Chola invasion led to the fall of the Sailendra Dynasty of Srivijaya and the Chola invasion also coincides with return voyage of the great Buddhist scholar Atiśa from Sumatra to India and Tibet in 1025. The expedition of Rajendra Chola I is mentioned in the corrupted form as Raja Chulan in the medieval Malay chronicle Sejarah Melaya, and Malay princes have names ending with Cholan or Chulan, such as

Raja Chulan of Perak history, ancient India and Indonesia enjoyed friendly and peaceful relations, therefore this Indian invasion is a unique event in Asian history. In the 9th and 10th centuries, Srivijaya maintained close relations with the Pala Empire in Bengal, and an 860 Nalanda inscription records that Maharaja Balaputra of Srivijaya dedicated a monastery at the Nalanda Mahavihara in Pala territory. The relation between Srivijaya and the Chola dynasty of southern India was friendly during the reign of Raja Raja Chola I. In 1006 CE a Srivijayan Maharaja from Sailendra dynasty — king Maravijayattungavarman — constructed the Chudamani Vihara in the port town of Nagapattinam.[14] However, during the reign of Rajendra Chola I the relations deteriorated as the Cholas attacked Srivijayan cities. The Cholas are known to have benefitted from both piracy and foreign trade. Sometimes Chola seafaring led to outright plunder and conquest as far as Southeast Asia.[16] While Srivijaya that controlled two major naval choke points; Malacca and Sunda Strait; at that time was a major trading empire that possess formidable naval forces. Malacca strait's northwest opening was controlled from Kedah on Peninsula side and from Pannai on the Sumatran side, while Malayu (Jambi) and Palembang controlled its southeast opening and also Sunda Strait. They practiced naval trade monopoly that forced any trade vessels that passed through their waters to call on their ports or otherwise being plundered. The reasons of this naval expedition are unclear with Nilakanta Sastri suggesting that the attack was probably caused by Srivijayan attempt to throw obstacles in the way of the Chola trade with the East (especially China), or more probably, a simple desire on the part of Rajendra to extend his digvijaya to the countries across the sea so well known to his subject at home, and therefore add luster to his crown.[17] Another theory suggests that the reasons for the invasion was probably motivated by geopolitics and diplomatic relations. King Suryavarman I of the Khmer Empire requested aid from Rajendra Chola I of the Chola dynasty against Tambralinga kingdom.[18] After learning of Suryavarman's alliance with Rajendra Chola, the Tambralinga kingdom requested aid from the Srivijaya king Sangrama Vijayatungavarman. This eventually led to the Chola Empire coming into conflict with the Srivijaya Empire. This alliance somewhat also had religious nuance, since both Chola and Khmer empire are Hindu Shivaist, while Tambralinga and Srivijaya are Mahayana Buddhist.

CHAPTER SIXTEEN

INVASION

A Siamese painting depicting the Chola raid on Kedah. The Chola raid against Srivijaya was a swift campaign that left Srivijaya unprepared. To sail from India to the Indonesian Archipelago, vessels from India sailed eastward across the Bay of Bengal and called at the ports of Lamuri in Aceh or Kedah in Malay peninsula before entering Strait of Malacca. But the Chola armada sailed directly to the Sumatran west coast. The port of Barus in the west coast of North Sumatra at that time belonged to Tamil trading guilds and served as a port to replenish after crossing the Indian Ocean. The Chola armada then continued to sail along Sumatra's west coast southward and sailed into Strait of Sunda. The Srivijaya navy guarded Kedah and surrounding areas on the northwest opening of the Malacca strait completely unaware that the Chola invasion was coming from the Sunda Strait in the south. The first Srivijayan city being raided was Palembang, the capital of Srivijaya empire. The unexpected attack led to the Cholas sacking the city and plundering the Kadatuan royal palace and monasteries. Thanjavur inscription states that Rajendra captured King Sangrama Vijayottunggavarman of Srivijaya and took a large heap of treasures including the Vidhyadara Torana, the jeweled 'war gate' of Srivijaya adorned with great splendor.

After plundering the royal palace of Palembang, the Cholas launched successive attacks on other Srivijayan ports including Malayu, Tumasik, Pannai and Kedah. The Chola invasion did not result in administration over defeated cities as the armies moved fast and plundered the Srivijayan cities. The Chola armada seems to have taken advantage of the Southeast Asian monsoon for moving from one port to another swiftly. The tactic of a fast-moving unexpected attack was probably the secret of Cholan success, since it did not allow the Srivijayan mandala to prepare the defences, reorganize themselves, provide assistance or to retaliate. The war ended with a victory for the Cholas and major losses for the Srivijaya Empire ending the Srivijaya maritime monopoly in the region.

CHAPTER SEVENTEEN

AFTERMATH

With the Maharaja Sangrama Vijayottunggavarman imprisoned and most of its cities destroyed, the leaderless Srivijaya mandala entered a period of chaos and confusion. The invasion marked the end of the Sailendra dynasty. According to the 15th-century Malay annals Sejarah Melayu, Rajendra Chola I after the successful naval raid in 1025 married Onang Kiu, the daughter of Vijayottunggavarman.This invasion forced Srivijaya to make peace with Javanese kingdom of Kahuripan. The peace deal was brokered by the exiled daughter of Vijayottunggavarman, a Srivijayan princess who managed to escape the destruction of Palembang and came to the court of King Airlangga in East Java. She also became the queen consort of Airlangga named Dharmaprasadottungadevi and in 1035, Airlangga constructed a Buddhist monastery named Srivijayasrama dedicated to his queen consort. Despite the devastation, Srivijaya mandala still survived as the Chola invasion ultimately failed to install direct administration over Srivijaya, since the invasion was short and only meant to plunder. Nevertheless, this invasion gravely weakened the Srivijayan hegemony and enabled the formation of regional kingdoms like Kahuripan and its successor, Kediri in Java based on agriculture rather than coastal and long-distance trade. Sri Deva was enthroned as the new king and the trading activities resumed. He sent an embassy to the court of China in 1028 CE. Although the invasion was not followed by direct Cholan occupation and the region was unchanged geographically, there were huge consequences in trade. Tamil traders encroached on the Srivijayan realm traditionally controlled by Malay traders and the Tamil guilds' influence increased on the Malay Peninsula and north coast of Sumatra. With the growing presence of Tamil guilds in the region, relations improved between Srivijaya and the Cholas. Chola nobles were accepted in Srivijaya court and in 1067 CE, a Chola prince named Divakara or Devakala was sent as a Srivijayan ambassador to the Imperial Court of China. The prince who was the nephew of Rajendra Chola later was enthroned in 1070 CE as Kulothunga Chola I. Later during the Kedah rebellion, Srivijaya asked the Cholas for help. In 1068 CE, Virarajendra Chola launched a naval raid to help Srivijaya reclaim Kedah. Virarajendra reinstated the Kedah king at the request of the Srivijayan Maharaja and Kedah accepted the Srivijayan sovereignty. In continuation of the decline, also marked by the resurgence of the Pandyan dynasty as the most powerful rulers in South India, a lack of a controlling central administration in its erstwhilePandyan territories prompted a number of claimants to the Pandya throne to cause a civil war in which the Sinhalas and the Cholas were involved by proxy. Details of the Pandyan civil war and the role played by the Cholas and Sinhalas, are present in the Mahavamsa as well as the Pallavarayanpettai Inscriptions.

OVERSEAS CONQUESTS

During the reign of Rajaraja Chola I and his successors Rajendra Chola I, Virarajendra Chola and Kulothunga Chola I the Chola armies invaded Sri Lanka, the Maldives and parts of Southeast Asia like Malaysia, Indonesia and Southern Thailand of the Srivijaya Empire in the 11th century. Rajaraja Chola I launched several naval campaigns that resulted in the capture of Sri Lanka, Maldives and the Malabar Coast. In 1025, Rajendra Chola launched naval raids on ports of Srivijaya and against the Burmese kingdom of Pegu. A Chola inscription states that he captured or plundered 14 places, which have been identified with Palembang, Tambralinga and Kedah among others. A second invasion was led by Virarajendra Chola, who conquered Kedah in Malaysia of Srivijaya in the late 11th century. Chola invasion ultimately failed to install direct administration over Srivijaya, since the invasion was short and only meant to plunder the wealth of Srivijaya. However, this invasion gravely weakened the Srivijayan hegemony and enabled the formation of regional kingdoms. Although the invasion was not followed by direct Cholan occupation and the region was unchanged geographically, there were huge consequences in trade. Tamil traders encroached on the Srivijayan realm traditionally controlled by Malay traders and the Tamil guilds' influence increased on the Malay Peninsula and north coast of Sumatra.

• 41 •

CHAPTER NINETEEN

DECLINE

The Cholas, under Rajaraja Chola III and later, his successor Rajendra Chola III, were quite weak and therefore, experienced continuous trouble. One feudatory, the Kadava chieftain Kopperunchinga I, even held Rajaraja Chola III as hostage for sometime. At the close of the 12th century, the growing influence of the Hoysalas replaced the declining Chalukyas as the main player in the Kannada country, but they too faced constant trouble from the Seunas and the Kalachuris, who were occupying Chalukya capital because those empires were their new rivals. So naturally, the Hoysalas found it convenient to have friendly relations with the Cholas from the time of Kulothunga Chola III, who had defeated Hoysala Veera Ballala II, who had subsequent marital relations with the Chola monarch. This continued during the time of Rajaraja Chola III the son and successor of Kulothunga Chola III.

The Hoysalas played a divisive role in the politics of the Tamil country during this period. They thoroughly exploited the lack of unity among the Tamil kingdoms and alternately supported one Tamil kingdom against the other thereby preventing both the Cholas and Pandyas from rising to their full potential. During the period of Rajaraja III, the Hoysalas sided with the Cholas and defeated the

Kadava chieftain Kopperunjinga and the Pandyas and established a presence in the Tamil country. Rajendra Chola III who succeeded Rajaraja III was a much better ruler who took bold steps to revive the Chola fortunes. He led successful expeditions to the north as attested by his epigraphs found as far as Cuddappah. He also defeated two Pandya princes one of whom was Maravarman Sundara Pandya II and briefly made the Pandyas submit to the Chola overlordship. The Hoysalas, under Vira Someswara, were quick to intervene and this time they sided with the Pandyas and repulsed the Cholas in order to counter the latter's revival.

The Pandyas in the south had risen to the rank of a great power who ultimately banished the Hoysalas from Malanadu or Kannada country, who were allies of the Cholas from Tamil country and the demise of the Cholas themselves ultimately was caused by the Pandyas in 1279. The Pandyas first steadily gained control of the Tamil country as well as territories in Sri Lanka, southern Chera country, Telugu country under Maravarman Sundara Pandiyan II and his able successor Jatavarman Sundara Pandyan before inflicting several defeats on the joint forces of the Cholas under Rajaraja Chola III, and the Hoysalas under Someshwara, his son Ramanatha The Pandyans gradually became major players in the Tamil country from 1215 and intelligently consolidated their position in Madurai-Rameswaram-Ilam-southern Chera country and Kanyakumari belt, and had been steadily increasing their territories in the Kaveri belt between Dindigul-Tiruchy-Karur-Satyamangalam as well as in the Kaveri Delta i.e., ThanjavurMayuram-Chidambaram-Vriddhachalam-Kanchi, finally marching all the way up to Arcot—Tirumalai-Nellore-Visayawadai-Vengi-Kalingam belt by

1250.

CHAPTER TWENTY

THE TERRITORY

According to Tamil tradition, the Chola country comprised the region that includes the modern-day Tiruchirapalli District, Tiruvarur District, Nagapattinam District, Ariyalur District, Perambalur district, Pudukkottai district, Thanjavur District in Tamil Nadu and Karaikal District. The river Kaveri and its tributaries dominate this landscape of generally flat country that gradually slopes towards the sea, unbroken by major hills or valleys. The river, which is also known as the Ponni (Golden) river, had a special place in the culture of Cholas. The annual floods in the Kaveri marked an occasion for celebration, known as Adiperukku, in which the whole nation took part. Kaveripoompattinam on the coast near the Kaveri delta was a major port town. Ptolemy knew of this, which he called Khaberis, and the other port town of Nagappattinam as the most important centres of Cholas. These two towns became hubs of trade and commerce and attracted many religious faiths, including Buddhism.[k] Roman ships found their way into these ports. Roman coins dating from the early centuries of the common era have been found near the Kaveri delta. The other major towns were Thanjavur, Uraiyur and Kudanthai, now known as Kumbakonam. After Rajendra Chola moved his capital to Gangaikonda Cholapuram, Thanjavur lost its importance.

THE GOVERMENT

In the age of the Cholas, the whole of South India was for the first time brought under a single government. The Cholas' system of government was monarchical, as in the Sangam age which was a form of government in which a person, the monarch, is head of state for life or until abdication. The political legitimacy and governing power of the monarch may vary from purely symbolic (crowned republic), to restricted (constitutional monarchy), to fully autocratic (absolute Monarchy) combining executive, legislative and judicial power. However, there was little in common between the local chiefdoms of the earlier period and the imperial-like states of Rajaraja Chola and his successors. Aside from the early capital at Thanjavur and the later on at Gangaikonda Cholapuram, Kanchipuram and Madurai were considered to be regional capitals in which occasional courts were held. The king was the supreme leader and a benevolent authoritarian. His administrative role consisted of issuing oral commands to responsible officers when representations were made to him.

Due to the lack of a legislature or a legislative system in the modern sense, the fairness of king's orders dependent on his morality and belief in Dharma. The Chola kings built temples and endowed them with great wealth. The temples acted not only as places of worship but also as centres of economic activity, benefiting the community as a whole. Some of the output of villages throughout the kingdom was given to temples that reinvested some of the wealth accumulated as loans to the settlements.. The Chola Dynasty was divided into several provinces called Mandalams which were further divided into Valanadus and these Valanadus were sub-divided into units called Kottams or Kutrams.

According to Kathleen Gough, during the Chola period the Vellalar were the "dominant secular aristocratic caste ... providing the courtiers, most of the army officers, the lower ranks of the kingdom's bureaucracy, and the upper layer of the peasantry". Vellalar is a generic Tamil term used primarily by various castes who traditionally pursued agriculture as a profession in the Indian states of Tamil Nadu, Kerala and northeastern parts of Sri Lanka. Some of the communities that identify themselves as a Vellalar are the numerically strong Arunattu Vellalar, Chozhia Vellalar, Karkarthar Vellalar, Kongu Vellalar, Thuluva Vellalar and Sri Lankan Vellalar. Despite being a relatively lowly group, they were dominant communities in Tamil agrarian societies for 600 years until the decline of the Chola empire in the 13th century, with their chieftains able to practise state-level political authority after winning the support and legitimisation of Brahmins and other higher-ranked communities with grants of land and honours Before the reign of Rajaraja Chola I huge parts of the Chola territory were ruled by hereditary lords and local princes who were in a loose alliance with the Chola rulers. Thereafter, until the reign of Vikrama Chola in 1133 CE when the Chola power was at its peak, these hereditary lords and local princes virtually vanished from the Chola records and were either replaced or turned into dependent officials. Through these dependent officials the administration was improved and the Chola kings were able to exercise a closer control over the different parts of the empire.

There was an expansion of the administrative structure, particularly from the reign of Rajaraja Chola I onwards. The government at this time had a large land revenue department, consisting of several tiers, which was largely concerned with maintaining accounts. The assessment and collection of revenue were undertaken by corporate bodies such as the ur, nadu, sabha, nagaram and sometimes by local chieftains who passed the revenue to the centre. During the reign of Rajaraja Chola I, the state initiated a massive project of land survey and assessment and there was a reorganisation of the empire into units known as valanadus. The order of the King was first communicated by the executive officer to the local authorities. Afterwards the records of the transaction was drawn up and attested by a number of witnesses who were either local magnates or government officers.

At local government level, every village was a self-governing unit. A number of villages constituted a larger entity known as a Kurram, Nadu or Kottam, depending on the area. A number of Kurrams constituted a valanadu. These structures underwent constant change and refinement throughout the Chola period. Justice was mostly a local matter in the Chola Empire; minor disputes were settled at the village level. Punishment for minor crimes were in the form of fines or a direction for the offender to donate to some charitable endowment. Even crimes such as manslaughter or murder were punished with fines. Crimes of the state, such as treason, were heard and decided by the king himself; the typical punishment in these cases was either execution or confiscation of property.

CHAPTER TWENTY-TWO

MILITARY

The Chola dynasty had a robust military, of which the king was the supreme commander. It had four elements, comprising the cavalry, the elephant corps, several divisions of infantry and a navy. There were regiments of bowmen and swordsmen while the swordsmen were the most permanent and dependable troops. The Chola army was spread all over the country and was stationed in local garrisons or military camps known as Kodagams. The elephants played a major role in the army and the dynasty had numerous war elephants. These carried houses or huge Howdahs on their backs, full of soldiers who shot arrows at long range and who fought with spears at close quarters.

The Chola rulers built several palaces and fortifications to protect their cities. The fortifications were mostly made up of bricks but other materials like stone, wood and mud were also used. According to the ancient Tamil text Silappadikaram, the Tamil kings defended their forts with catapults that threw stones, huge cauldrons of boiling water or molten lead, and hooks, chains and traps.

The soldiers of the Chola dynasty used weapons such as swords, bows, javelins, spears and shields which were made up of steel. Particularly the famous Wootz steel, which has a long history in south India dating back to the period before the Christian era, seems also be used to produce weapons. The army consisted of people from different castes but the warriors of the Kaikolar and Vellalar castes played a prominent role. The Chola navy was the zenith of ancient India sea power. It played a vital role in the expansion of the empire, including the conquest of the Ceylon islands and naval raids on Srivijaya. The navy grew both in size and status during the medieval Cholas reign. The Chola admirals commanded much respect and prestige. The navy commanders also acted as diplomats in some instances. From 900 to 1100, the navy had grown from a small backwater entity to that of a potent power projection and diplomatic symbol in all of Asia, but was gradually reduced in significance when the Cholas fought land battles subjugating the Chalukyas of the AndhraKannada area in South India.

CHAPTER TWENTY-THREE

SILAMBAM

A martial art called Silambam was patronised by the Chola rulers. Ancient and medieval Tamil texts mention different forms of martial traditions but the ultimate expression of the loyalty of the warrior to his commander was a form of martial suicide called Navakandam. The medieval Kalingathu Parani text, which celebrates the victory of Kulothunga Chola I and his general in the battle for Kalinga, describes the practice in detail. Oral folklore traces Silambam back several thousand years to the siddhar (enlightened sage) Agastya. While on his way to Vellimalai, Agastya discussed Hindu philosophy with an old man he met, said to be the god Murugan in disguise. The old man taught him of kundalini yoga and how to focus prana through the body's nadi (channels). Agastya practiced this method of meditation and eventually compiled three texts on palm leaves based on the god's teachings. One of these texts was the Kampu Sutra (Staff Classic) which was said to record advanced fighting theories in verse. These poems and the art they described were allegedly passed on to other Siddha of the Agastmuni akhara (Agastya school) and eventually formed the basis of Silambam, siddha medicine, and also influenced the southern style of kalaripayattu. Silambam became more common in Southeast Asia than its native India where it was banned by the British rulers.

Silambam name has made its historical first time appearance in the world eyes as the committee of United Nations Assembly recommends Silambam Asia for United Nations status for representing Asia Continent. Occasion held at the United Nations Headquarters in New York, United States on January 21, 2019 whereby China-Taipei government representatives arised border conflicts in ancient recording pertaining Silambam and requesting organisation of Silambam Asia to resolve prior to internal committee clearance request. On January 30, 2019 concluded substantive work as the Committee recommended Silambam Asia for Special Status in the United Nations

CHAPTER TWENTY-FOUR

THE ECONOMY

Land revenue and trade tax were the main source of income. The Chola rulers issued their coins in gold, silver and copper. The Chola economy was based on three tiers—at the local level, agricultural settlements formed the foundation to commercial towns nagaram, which acted as redistribution centres for externally produced items bound for consumption in the local economy and as sources of products made by nagaram artisans for the international trade. At the top of this economic pyramid were the elite merchant groups (samayam) who organised and dominated the regions international maritime trade.

One of the main articles which were exported to foreign countries were cotton cloth. Uraiyur, the capital of the early Chola rulers, was a famous centre for cotton textiles which were praised by Tamil poets. The Chola rulers actively encouraged the weaving industry and derived revenue from it. During this period the weavers started to organise themselves into guilds. The weavers had their own residential sector in all towns. The most important weaving communities in early medieval times were the Saliyar and Kaikolar. During the Chola period silk weaving attained a high degree and Kanchipuram became one of the main centres for silk. Metal crafts reached its zenith during the

10th to 11th centuries because the Chola rulers like Chembian Maadevi extended their patronage to metal craftsmen. Wootz steel was a major export item. The farmers occupied one of the highest positions in society. These were the Vellalar community who formed the nobility or the landed aristocracy of the country and who were economically a powerful group Agriculture was the principal occupation for many people. Besides the landowners, there were others dependent on agriculture.The Vellalar community was the dominant secular aristocratic caste under the Chola rulers, providing the courtiers, most of the army officers, the lower ranks of the bureaucracy and the upper layer of the peasantry.

In almost all villages the distinction between persons paying the land-tax (iraikudigal) and those who did not was clearly established. There was a class of hired day-labourers who assisted in agricultural operations on the estates of other people and received a daily wage. All cultivable land was held in one of the three broad classes of tenure which can be distinguished as peasant proprietorship called vellan-vagai, service tenure and eleemosynary tenure resulting from charitable gifts.

The vellan-vagai was the ordinary ryotwari village of modern times, having direct relations with the government and paying a land-tax liable to revision from time to time. The vellan-vagai villages fell into two broad classes- one directly remitting a variable annual revenue to the state and the other paying dues of a more or less fixed character to the public institutions like temples to which they were assigned.The prosperity of an agricultural country depends to a large extent on the facilities provided for irrigation. Apart from sinking wells and excavating tanks, the Chola rulers threw mighty stone dams across the Kaveri and other rivers, and cut out channels to distribute water over large tracts of land. Rajendra Chola I dug near his capital an artificial lake, which was filled with water from the Kolerun and the Vellar rivers. There existed a brisk internal trade in several articles carried on by the organised mercantile corporations in various parts of the country. The metal industries and the jewellers art had reached a high degree of excellence. The manufacture of sea-salt was carried on under government supervision and control. Trade was carried on by merchants organised in guilds. The guilds described sometimes by the terms nanadesis were a powerful autonomous corporation of merchants which visited different countries in the course of their trade. They had their own mercenary army for the protection of their merchandise. There were also local organisations of merchants called "nagaram" in big centres of trade like Kanchipuram and Mamallapuram.

CHAPTER TWENTY-FIVE

HOSPITALS

Hospitals were maintained by the Chola kings, whose government gave lands for that purpose. The Tirumukkudal inscription shows that a hospital was named after Vira Chola. Many diseases were cured by the doctors of the hospital, which was under the control of a chief physician who was paid annually 80 Kalams of paddy, 8 Kasus and a grant of land. Apart from the doctors, other remunerated staff included a nurse, barber (who performed minor operations) and a waterman. The Chola queen Kundavai also established a hospital at Tanjavur and gave land for the perpetual maintenance of it.

CHAPTER TWENTY-SIX

SOCIETY

During the Chola period several guilds, communities and castes emerged. The guild was one of the most significant institutions of south India and merchants organised themselves into guilds. The best known of these were the Manigramam and Ayyavole guilds though other guilds such as Anjuvannam and Valanjiyar were also in existence.The farmers occupied one of the highest positions in society. These were the Vellalar community who formed the nobility or the landed aristocracy of the country and who were economically a powerful group. The Vellalar community was the dominant secular aristocratic caste under the Chola rulers, providing the courtiers, most of the army officers, the lower ranks of the bureaucracy and the upper layer of the peasantry. The Vellalar were also sent to northern Sri Lanka by the Chola rulers as settlers. The Ulavar community were working in the field which was associated with agriculture and the peasants were known as Kalamar. The Kaikolar community were weavers and merchants but they also maintained armies. During the Chola period they had predominant trading and military roles. During the reign of the Imperial Chola rulers (10th-13th century) there were major changes in the temple administration and land ownership. There was more involvement of non-Brahmin elements in the temple administration. This can be attributed to the shift in money power. Skilled classes like the weavers and the merchant-class had become prosperous. Land ownership was no longer a privilege of the Brahmins (priest caste) and the Vellalar land owners. There is little information on the size and the density of the population during the Chola reign. The stability in the core Chola region enabled the people to lead a productive and contented life. However, there were reports of widespread famine caused by natural calamities. The quality of the inscriptions of the regime indicates a high level of literacy and education. The text in these inscriptions was written by court poets and engraved by talented artisans. Education in the contemporary sense was not considered important; there is circumstantial evidence to suggest that some village councils organised schools to teach the basics of reading and writing to children, although there is no evidence of systematic educational system for the masses. Vocational education was through hereditary training in which the father passed on his skills to his sons. Tamil was the medium of education for the masses; Religious monasteries (matha or gatika) were centres of learning and received government support.

CHAPTER TWENTY-SEVEN

FORIEGN TRADE

The relationship between the Chinese and Cholas dates back to second century BC. Ancient Chinese scholar Ban Gu had told that China had sent its ambassador to the court of the Cholas.[1] Ban Gu in his work the Book of Han (Ch'ien Han Shu) had written that he had seen many unprecedented objects which are unseen at China, at the city of kuvangtche. Berend, an acoustics expert, annotates that the city named by Ban Gu is analogous with the ancient Chola city kanchi (the present day's city of Kancheepuram at Tamil Nadu, India). This proves the relationship of Kanchi with China.

CHAPTER TWENTY-EIGHT

THE COINS

Arrays of ancient Chinese coins have been found in recent years at the place which is considered to be the homeland of the Cholas (i.e. the present Thanjavur, Tiruvarur and Pudukkottai districts of Tamil Nadu, India), which confirms the trade and the commercial relationship which existed between the Cholas and the Chinese.

PLACE   NO.OF OTHER DETAILS
COINS

<u>Olayakkunnam</u> *323* These coins belong to 142-126 BC. This village is situated in Pattukkottai taluk in Pudukkottai district of Tamil Nadu, India

<u>Thaalikkottai</u>*1822* This village is situated in Mannargudi taluk in Tiruvarur district of Tamil Nadu, India

CHAPTER TWENTY-NINE

INTERNATIONAL RELATIONS

The later Cholas too continued to maintain a healthy relationship with the Chinese. During the reign of Rajendra Chola I (i.e. 1016–1033 AD) and Kulothunga Chola I (i.e. in 1077 AD), commercial and political diplomats were sent to China.

The Cholas excelled in foreign trade and maritime activity, extending their influence overseas to China and Southeast Asia.. Towards the end of the 9th century, southern India had developed extensive maritime and commercial activity.[162] The south Indian guilds played a major role in interregional and overseas trade. The best known of these were the Manigramam and Ayyavole guilds who followed the conquering Chola armies.[152] The encouragement by the Chola court furthered the expansion of Tamil merchant associations such as the Ayyavole and Manigramam guilds into Southeast Asia and China. The Cholas, being in possession of parts of both the west and the east coasts of peninsular India, were at the forefront of these ventures. The Tang dynasty of China, the Srivijaya empire under the Sailendras, and the Abbasid Kalifat at Baghdad were the main trading partners.

Some credit for the emergence of a world market must also go to the dynasty. It played a significant role in linking the markets of China to the rest of the world. The market structure and economic policies of the Chola dynasty were more conducive to a large-scale, cross-regional market trade than those enacted by the Chinese Song Dynasty. A Chola record gives their rationale for engagement in foreign trade: "Make the merchants of distant foreign countries who import elephants and good horses attach to yourself by providing them with villages and decent dwellings in the city, by affording them daily audience, presents and allowing them profits. Then those articles will never go to your enemies. Song dynasty reports record that an embassy from Chulian (Chola) reached the Chinese court in 1077, and that the king of the Chulian at the time, Kulothunga I, was called Ti-hua-kia-lo. This embassy was a trading venture and was highly profitable to the visitors, who returned with copper coins in exchange for articles of tribute, including glass and spices. Probably, the motive behind Rajendra's expedition to Srivijaya was the protection of the merchants' interests.

CHAPTER THIRTY

CANALS AND WATER TANKS

There was tremendous agrarian expansion during the rule of the imperial Chola Dynasty (c. 900- 1270 AD) all over Tamil Nadu and particularly in the Kaveri Basin. Most of the canals of the Kaveri River belongs to this period e.g., Uyyakondan canal, Rajendran vaykkal, Sembian Mahadegvi vaykkal. There was a well-developed and highly efficient system of water management from the village level upwards. The increase in the royal patronage and also the number of devadana and bramadeya lands which increased the role of the temples and village assemblies in the field. Committees like eri-variyam (tank-committee) and totta-variam (garden committees) were active as also the temples with their vast resources in land, men and money. The water tanks that came up during the Chola period are too many to be listed here. But a few most outstanding may be briefly mentioned. Rajendra Chola built a huge tank named Solagangam in his capital city Gangaikonda Solapuram and was described as the liquid pillar of victory. About 16 miles long, it was provided with sluices and canals for irrigating the lands in the neighbouring areas. Another very large lake of this period, which even today seems an important source of irrigation was the Viranameri near Kattumannarkoil in South Arcot district founded by Parantaka Chola. Other famous lakes of this period are Madurantakam, Sundrachola Peratiyar, Kundavai-Peratiyar (after a Chola queen).

Under the Cholas, the Tamil country reached new heights of excellence in art, religion, music and literature. In all of these spheres, the Chola period marked the culmination of movements that had begun in an earlier age under the Pallavas. Monumental architecture in the form of majestic temples and sculpture in stone and bronze reached a finesse never before achieved in India. The Chola conquest of Kadaram (Kedah) and Srivijaya, and their continued commercial contacts with the Chinese Empire, enabled them to influence the local cultures. Examples of the Hindu cultural influence found today throughout the Southeast Asia owe much to the legacy of the Cholas. For example, the great temple complex at Prambanan in Indonesia exhibit a number of similarities with the South Indian architecture. According to the Malay chronicle Sejarah Melayu, the rulers of the Malacca sultanate claimed to be descendants of the kings of the Chola Empire. Chola rule is remembered in Malaysia today as many princes there have names ending with Cholan or Chulan, one such being Raja Chulan, the Raja of Perak.

CHAPTER THIRTY-ONE

ART AND ARCHITECTURE

The Cholas continued the temple-building traditions of the Pallava dynasty and contributed significantly to the Dravidian temple design.[They built a number of Shiva temples along the banks of the river Kaveri. The template for these and future temples was formulated by Aditya I and Parantaka. The Chola temple architecture has been appreciated for its magnificence as well as delicate workmanship, ostensibly following the rich traditions of the past bequeathed to them by the Pallava Dynasty. Architectural historian James Fergusson says that "the Chola artists conceived like giants and finished like jewelers".A new development in Chola art that characterised the Dravidian architecture in later times was the addition of a huge gateway called gopuram to the enclosure of the temple, which had gradually taken its form and attained maturity under the Pandya Dynasty. The Chola school of art also spread to Southeast Asia and influenced the architecture and art of Southeast Asia. Temple building received great impetus from the conquests and the genius of Rajaraja Chola and his son Rajendra Chola I. The maturity and grandeur to which the Chola architecture had evolved found expression in the two temples of Thanjavur and Gangaikondacholapuram. The magnificent Shiva temple of Thanjavur, completed around 1009, is a fitting memorial to the material achievements of the time of Rajaraja. The largest and tallest of all Indian temples of its time, it is at the apex of South Indian architecture. The temple of Gangaikondacholisvaram at Gangaikondacholapuram, the creation of Rajendra Chola, was intended to excel its predecessor. Completed around 1030, only two decades after the temple at Thanjavur and in the same style, the greater elaboration in its appearance attests the more affluent state of the Chola Empire under Rajendra. The Brihadisvara Temple, the temple of Gangaikondacholisvaram and the Airavatesvara Temple at Darasuram were declared as World Heritage Sites by the UNESCO and are referred to as the Great living Chola temples. The Chola period is also remarkable for its sculptures and bronzes. Among the existing specimens in museums around the world and in the temples of South India may be seen many fine figures of Shiva in various forms, such as Vishnu and his consort Lakshmi, and the Shaivite saints. Though conforming generally to the iconographic conventions established by long tradition, the sculptors worked with great freedom in the 11th and the 12th centuries to achieve a classic grace and grandeur. The best example of this can be seen in the form of Nataraja the divine dancer

MAJOR BATTLES

He led the famous campaign against the Western Chalukyas and succeeded in invading Kollipakkai or modern-Kulpak in the north of Hyderabad. 47 While his father was successful in capturing the northern part of Sri Lanka, he went ahead in annexing the entire island in 1017, defeating the Sinhala king, Mahinda V and imprisoning him in the Chola Country, where he died in captivity.He fought the Western Chalukya king, Jayasimha II, in the Battle of Maski, in 1021, who attempted to control the Eastern Chalukyas of Vengi by supporting Vijayaditya VII and sending his nephew, Rajaraja Narendra, into exile. In 1025, he invaded Sangrama Vijayatungavarman's Srivijaya kingdom, imprisoning him and capturing its capital Kadaram, Pannai (present-Sumatra), Kedah and Malaiyur.

CHAPTER THIRTY-THREE

ACHIEVEMENTS

He got a large artificial lake, measuring 16 miles long and 3 miles wide, constructed at his capital Gangaikondacholapuram, which is, till date, one of the largest manmade lakes in India. Being a devout and religious ruler, he got most of the brick-structured temples in his empire converted into stone shrines.

CHAPTER THIRTY-FOUR

PERSONAL LIFE AND LEGACY

He was believed to have had several queens, some of them being Mukkokilan, Arindhavan Madevi, Tribuvana or Vananan Mahadeviar, Panchavan Mahadevi, and Viramadevi, who committed sati upon his death in 1044.He was succeeded by three of his sons – Rajadhiraja Chola, Rajendra Chola II and Virarajendra Chola.He had two daughters – Pranaar Arul Mozhi Nangai and Ammanga Devi, who was married to Eastern Chalukya king Rajaraja Narendra and bore the first Chalukya Chola emperor, Kulothunga Chola I. A number of medieval inscriptions written in Tamil language and script that have been found in Southeast Asia and China, mainly in Sumatra and peninsular Thailand. These texts arose directly from trade links between south India and certain parts of Southeast Asia and China, which involved the residence in those regions of Tamil-speaking Indians. Several of these overseas Tamil inscriptions mention well-known medieval Indian merchant associations.

" A good number of Tamil inscriptions, as well as Hindu and Buddhist icons emanating from South India, have been found in Southeast Asia (and even in parts of south China).

On the Malay Peninsula, inscriptions have been found at Takuapa, not far from the Vishnuite statues of Khao Phra Narai in Southern Thailand. It is a short inscription indicating that an artificial lake named Avani-naranam was dug by Nangur-Udaiyan, which is the name of an individual who possessed a military fief at Nangur, being famous for his abilities as a warrior, and that the lake was placed under the protection of the members of the Manikkiramam (which according to K. A. Nilakanta Sastri, was a merchant guild) living in the military camp. Since Avani-narayana is a surname of the Pallava King Nandivarman III who reigned from 826 to 849, we can deduce the approximate date of this inscription. In the capital of Tabralinga there is a sanctuary in which there is a bronze image of Ganesa bearing a Tamil inscription Majapisedesa in modern characters. In ancient Kedah there is an important and unmistakably Hindu settlement which has been known for about a century now from the discoveries reported by Col. Low and has recently been subjected to a fairly exhaustive investigation by Dr. Quaritch Wales. Dr. Wales investigated no fewer than thirty sites round about Kedah.

The results attained show that this site was in continuous occupation by people who came under strong South Indian influences, Buddhist and Hindu, for centuries. An inscribed stone bar, rectangular in shape, bears the ye-dharmma formula in South Indian characters of the 4th century AD, thus proclaiming the Buddhist character of the shrine near the find-spot (site I) of which only the basement survives. It is inscribed on three faces in Pallava script, or Vatteluttu rounded writing of the 6th century AD, possibly earlier. An inscription in the Tamil language, the Lobu Tua Inscription dated 1088 AD, has been found on the western coast of Sumatra island at Lobu Tua, North

Sumatra province, Indonesia. It was erected by a Tamil merchant guild, the Ayyavole 500 ("the 500 of the thousand directions") which enjoyed the patronage of the Chola rulers. The inscription mentions the guild as "having met at the velapuram in Varocu". "Varocu" is Barus, an ancient port located not far from Lobu Tua, which had played a major role in the camphor and benzoin trade since the 9th century.

These valuable products were in high demand in China, India and the Middle East and came from the forests in the northern Sumatra hinterland. From there, they were brought to Barus and exported. Tamil were among the foreign merchants who would come to Barus and buy the camphor and benzoin from local traders. In 1017 and 1025, the Chola kings had sent fleets to raid ports controlled by Sriwijaya in the Malacca Straits. After these successful attacks, the Chola seem to have been in a position to intervene in the region for the rest of the 11th century. This allowed for an increased presence of Tamil merchant guilds in Sumatra. Inscriptions: In the ancient city of Tanjore (Thanjavur - ancient name) in Tamil Nadu are inscriptions dating from 1030. which contain a list of the ports in the Malacca Strait raided by a fleet sent by King Rajendra Chola I. A large stone makara found in Jambi province in Sumatra, dated 1064 AD, bears testimony to the reemergence of a significant power in Jambi, with a strong link to Java, in the 11th century. In 1025, Rajendra Chola I or Raja Ranganathan, the Chola king from Tamil Nadu in South India, launched naval raids on the city-state of Srivijaya in maritime Southeast Asia, and conquered Kadaram (modern Kedah) from Srivijaya and occupied it for some time. Rajendra's overseas expedition against Srivijaya was a unique event in India's history and its otherwise peaceful relations with the states of Southeast Asia. Several places in present day Malaysia and Indonesia were invaded by Rajendra Chola I of the Chola dynasty. The Chola invasion furthered the expansion of Tamil merchant associations such as the Manigramam, Ayyavole and Ainnurruvar into Southeast Asia.

The Chola invasion led to the fall of the Sailendra Dynasty of Srivijaya and the Chola invasion also coincides with return voyage of the great Buddhist scholar Atiśa from Sumatra to India and Tibet in 1025. The expedition of Rajendra Chola I is mentioned in the corrupted form as Raja Chulan in the medieval Malay chronicle Sejarah Melaya, and Malay princes have names ending with Cholan or Chulan, such as Raja Chulan of Perak. Throughout most of their shared history, ancient India and Indonesia enjoyed friendly and peaceful relations, therefore this Indian invasion is a unique event in Asian history. In the 9th and 10th centuries, Srivijaya maintained close relations with the Pala Empire in Bengal, and an 860 Nalanda inscription records that Maharaja Balaputra of Srivijaya dedicated a monastery at the Nalanda Mahavihara in Pala territory. The relation between Srivijaya and the Chola dynasty of southern India was friendly during the reign of Raja Raja Chola I. In 1006 CE a Srivijayan Maharaja from Sailendra dynasty — king Maravijayattungavarman — constructed the Chudamani Vihara in the port town of Nagapattinam. However, during the reign of Rajendra Chola I the relations deteriorated as the Cholas attacked Srivijayan cities. The Cholas are known to have benefitted from both piracy and foreign trade. Sometimes Chola seafaring led to outright plunder and conquest as far as Southeast Asia.

While Srivijaya that controlled two major naval choke points; Malacca and Sunda Strait; at that time was a major trading empire that possess formidable naval forces. Malacca strait's northwest opening was controlled from Kedah on Peninsula side and from Pannai on the Sumatran side, while Malayu (Jambi) and Palembang controlled its southeast opening and also Sunda Strait. They practiced naval trade monopoly that forced any trade vessels that passed through their waters to call on their ports or otherwise being plundered. The reasons of this naval expedition are unclear with Nilakanta Sastri suggesting that the attack was probably caused by Srivijayan attempt to throw obstacles in the way of the Chola trade with the East (especially China), or more probably, a simple desire on the part of Rajendra to extend his digvijaya to the countries across the sea so well known to his subject at home, and therefore add luster to his crown.

Another theory suggests that the reasons for the invasion was probably motivated by geopolitics and diplomatic relations. King Suryavarman I of the Khmer Empire requested aid from Rajendra Chola I of the Chola dynasty against Tambralinga kingdom. After learning of Suryavarman's alliance with Rajendra Chola, the Tambralinga kingdom requested aid from the Srivijaya king Sangrama Vijayatungavarman. This eventually led to the Chola Empire coming into conflict with the Srivijaya Empire. This alliance somewhat also had religious nuance, since both Chola and Khmer empire are Hindu Shivaist, while Tambralinga and Srivijaya are Mahayana Buddhist. The Chola raid against Srivijaya was a swift campaign that left Srivijaya unprepared. To sail from India to the Indonesian Archipelago, vessels from India sailed eastward across the Bay of Bengal and called at the ports of Lamuri in Aceh or Kedah in Malay peninsula before entering Strait of Malacca. But the Chola armada sailed directly to the Sumatran west coast.

The port of Barus in the west coast of North Sumatra at that time belonged to Tamil trading guilds and served as a port to replenish after crossing the Indian Ocean. The Chola armada then continued to sail along Sumatra's west coast southward and sailed into Strait of Sunda. The Srivijaya navy guarded Kedah and surrounding areas on the northwest opening of the Malacca strait completely unaware that the Chola invasion was coming from the Sunda Strait in the south. The first Srivijayan city being raided was Palembang, the capital of Srivijaya empire. The unexpected attack led to the Cholas sacking the city and plundering the Kadatuan royal palace and monasteries. Thanjavur inscription states that Rajendra captured King Sangrama Vijayottunggavarman of Srivijaya and took a large heap of treasures including the Vidhyadara Torana, the jeweled 'war gate' of Srivijaya adorned with great splendor. After plundering the royal palace of Palembang, the Cholas launched successive attacks on other Srivijayan ports including Malayu, Tumasik, Pannai and Kedah. The Chola invasion did not result in administration over defeated cities as the armies moved fast and plundered the Srivijayan cities. The Chola armada seems to have taken advantage of the Southeast Asian monsoon for moving from one port to another swiftly. The tactic of a fast-moving unexpected attack was probably the secret of Cholan success, since it did not allow the Srivijayan mandala to prepare the defences, reorganize themselves, provide assistance or to retaliate.The war ended with a victory for the Cholas and major losses for the Srivijaya Empire ending the Srivijaya maritime monopoly in the region.

CHAPTER THIRTY-FIVE

REPURCUSSION

With the Maharaja Sangrama Vijayottunggavarman imprisoned and most of its cities destroyed, the leaderless Srivijaya mandala entered a period of chaos and confusion. The invasion marked the end of the Sailendra dynasty. According to the 15th-century Malay annals Sejarah Melayu, Rajendra Chola I after the successful naval raid in 1025 married Onang Kiu, the daughter of Vijayottunggavarman. This invasion forced Srivijaya to make peace with Javanese kingdom of Kahuripan. The peace deal was brokered by the exiled daughter of Vijayottunggavarman, a Srivijayan princess who managed to escape the destruction of Palembang and came to the court of King Airlangga in East Java. She also became the queen consort of Airlangga named Dharmaprasadottungadevi and in 1035, Airlangga constructed a Buddhist monastery named Srivijayasrama dedicated to his queen consort. Despite the devastation, Srivijaya mandala still survived as the Chola invasion ultimately failed to install direct administration over Srivijaya, since the invasion was short and only meant to plunder.

Nevertheless, this invasion gravely weakened the Srivijayan hegemony and enabled the formation of regional kingdoms like Kahuripan and its successor, Kediri in Java based on agriculture rather than coastal and long-distance trade. Sri Deva was enthroned as the new king and the trading activities resumed. He sent an embassy to the court of China in 1028 CE. Although the invasion was not followed by direct Cholan occupation and the region was unchanged geographically, there were huge consequences in trade. Tamil traders encroached on the Srivijayan realm traditionally controlled by Malay traders and the Tamil guilds' influence increased on the Malay Peninsula and north coast of Sumatra.

With the growing presence of Tamil guilds in the region, relations improved between Srivijaya and the Cholas. Chola nobles were accepted in Srivijaya court and in 1067 CE, a Chola prince named Divakara or Devakala was sent as a Srivijayan ambassador to the Imperial Court of China. The prince who was the nephew of Rajendra Chola later was enthroned in 1070 CE as Kulothunga Chola I. Later during the Kedah rebellion, Srivijaya asked the Cholas for help. In 54 1068 CE, Virarajendra Chola launched a naval raid to help Srivijaya reclaim Kedah, Virarajendra reinstated the Kedah king at the request of the Srivijayan Maharaja and Kedah accepted the Srivijayan sovereignty.